My Own True Name

Also by Pat Mora

Poetry

Agua Santa / Holy Water

Aunt Carmen's Book of Practical Saints

Borders

Chants

Communion

Prose

House of Houses

Nepantla: Essays from the Land in the Middle

For Children

Agua, Agua, Agua

A Birthday Basket for Tía /
Una canasta de cumpleaños para Tía

Confetti: Poems for Children

Delicious Hullabaloo / *Pachanga deliciosa*

The Desert Is My Mother / *El desierto es mi madre*

The Gift of the Poinsettia / *El regalo de la flor de Nochebuena*
(with Charles Ramírez Berg)

Listen to the Desert / *Oye al desierto*

Pablo's Tree

The Race of Toad and Deer

The Rainbow Tulip

This Big Sky

Tomás and the Library Lady /
Tomás y la señora de la biblioteca

Uno, Dos, Tres: One, Two, Three

My Own True Name

New and Selected Poems for Young Adults,
1984-1999

Pat Mora

With Line Drawings by Anthony Accardo

PIÑATA BOOKS
ARTE PÚBLICO PRESS
HOUSTON, TEXAS
2000

This volume is made possible through grants from the National Endowment for the Arts (a federal agency), Andrew W. Mellon Foundation, and the City of Houston through The Cultural Arts Council of Houston, Harris County.

Piñata Books are full of surprises!

Piñata Books
An Imprint of Arte Público Press
University of Houston
452 Cullen Performance Hall
Houston, Texas 77204-2004

Cover illustration and design by Anthony Accardo

Mora, Pat.
  My own true name: new and selected poems for young adults, 1984–1999 / by Pat Mora.
    p. cm.
  Summary: More than sixty poems, some with Spanish translations, include such titles as "The Young Sor Juana," "Graduation Morning," "Border Town 1938," "Legal Alien."
  ISBN-10: 1-55885-292-1 (trade pbk. : alk. paper)
  ISBN-13: 978-1-55885-292-1
  1. Mexican Americans—Poetry. 2. Young adults poetry, American. [1. Mexican Americans—Poetry. 2. American poetry.]   I. Title.
PS3563.O73 M9 2000
811′.54—dc21
                                        00-023969
                                          CIP

Some of the poems in this book previously appeared in *Chants, Borders,* and *Communion* (all published by Arte Público Press).

6 7 8 9 0 1 2 3 4 5   10 9 8 7 6 5 4

To young writers of all shapes, colors, and sizes:
May you write many surprising poems.

And to the staff of Arte Público Press,
who have treated me so kindly through the years.

Contents

Blooms

Thorns

Roots

Dear Fellow Writer

Dear Fellow Writer,

A blank piece of paper can be exciting and intimidating. Probably every writer knows both reactions well. I know I do. I wanted to include a letter to you in this book because I wish I could talk to you individually. I'd say: Listen to your inside self, your private voice. Respect your thoughts and feelings and ideas. You—yes, you—play with sounds. With language(s), explore the wonder of being alive.

Living hurts, so sometimes we write about a miserable date, a friend who betrayed us, the death of a parent. Some days, though, we're so full of joy we feel like a kite. We can fly! Whether we write for ourselves or to share our words, we discover ourselves when we truly write: when we dive below the surface. It's never easy to really reveal ourselves in school, but remember that writing is practice. Without practice, you will never learn to hear and sing your own unique song.

I have always been a reader which is the best preparation for becoming a writer. When I was in grade school in El Paso, Texas (where I was born), I read comic books and mysteries and magazines and library books. I was soaking up language.

I've always liked to write, too—but I was a mother before I began to create regular time for my writing. Was it that I didn't think that I had anything important to say? Was it that I didn't believe that I could say anything that well? Was it that when I was in school we never studied a writer who was like me—bilingual, a Mexican American— and so somehow I decided that "people like me" couldn't be writers?

I have a large poster of an American Indian storyteller right above my desk. Children are climbing all over her, just as my sisters and my brother and I climbed over *nuestra tía,* our aunt, Ignacia Delgado, the aunt we called Lobo. She was our storyteller. Who is yours? Would you like to be a storyteller? Would you like to write or paint or draw or sing your stories?

I became a writer because words give me so much pleasure that I have always wanted to sink my hands and heart into them, to see what

1

I can create, what will rise up, what will appear on the page. I've learned that some writers are quiet and shy, others noisy, other just plain obnoxious. Some like enchiladas and others like sushi; some like rap and others like *rancheras*. Some write quickly, and some are as slow as an elderly man struggling up a steep hill on a windy day.

I'll tell you a few of our secrets.

The first is that we all read. Some of us like mysteries and some of us like memoirs, but writers are readers. We're curious to see what others are doing with words, but—what is more important—we like what happens to us when we open a book, how we journey into the pages.

Another secret is that we write often. We don't just talk about writing. We sit by ourselves inside or outside, writing at airports or on kitchen tables, even on napkins.

We're usually nosy and very good at eavesdropping. Just ask my three children! And writers are collectors. We collect facts and phrases and stories: the names of cacti, the word for *cheese* in many languages.

In the last twenty years, I've spent more and more time writing my own books for children and adults. I have received many rejections and will probably receive many more, darn it. I just keep writing—and revising. Revising is now one of my favorite parts of being a writer, though I didn't always feel that way. I enjoy taking what I've written—a picture or a book or a poem—and trying to make the writing better, by changing words or rhythm. Sometimes by starting over!

Writing is my way of knowing myself better, of hearing myself, of discovering what is important to me and what makes me sad, what makes me different, what makes me *me*—of discovering my own true name. And writing makes me less lonely. I have all these words in English and Spanish whispering or sometimes shouting at me, just waiting for me to put them to work, to combine them so that they leap over mountains on small hooves or slip down to the sandy bottom of the silent sea.

And you? Maybe these poems—taken from my collections *Chants, Borders,* and *Communion,* along with some new poems written for this book, for you—will tempt you to write your own poems about a special person or a special place, about a gray fear or a green hope. What are your blooms, your thorns, your roots?

Remember, my friend, never speak badly of your writing. Never make fun of it. Bring your inside voice out and let us hear you on the page. Come, join the serious and sassy family of writers.

Pat Mora

Blooms

A Secret

The clever twist
is pouring the tears
into a tall, black hat
waving a sharp No. 2 pencil
slowly over the blue echoes
then gently, gently
pulling out
a bloomin' poem.

Mango Juice

Eating mangoes
on a stick
is laughing
as gold juice
slides down
your chin
melting manners,
as mangoes slip
through your lips
sweet but biting

is hitting piñatas
blindfolded and spinning
away from the blues
and grays

is tossing
fragile *cascarones*
on your love's hair,
confetti teasing him
to remove his shoes
his mouth open
and laughing
as you glide
more mango in,
cool rich flesh
of México
music teasing
you to strew
streamers on trees
and cactus

teasing the wind
to stream through
your hair blooming
with confetti
and butterflies

your toes warm
in the sand.

Line 16: Eggshells emptied of their yolk, then filled with confetti and painted,
for tossing and breaking open during celebrations.

First Love

Her brown eyes circle
round me, circle
though she weaves
faraway by a fire
her eyes dart round me
like gold butterflies
   wherever I look
   wherever I run
they chase me like
I chased her round
creosote, circling boulders
her laugh light as dandelion
plumes.

Now her eyes play
tricks, hover
   as I sketch in the sand
   as I scramble to my secret place
  hover
   as I slowly paint two eyes
   on a cave with ochre and
   yucca brush.

Below, my laughing friends
wrestle, race, call my name,
but I hide watching her
eyes circle, circle.

Maybe

if I stretch myself tall
as a tree, if I sway
and pull my stomach in
until it touches my spine
and curl my hair into a river
of light, if I borrow
my sister's dress that whispers
when I glide without touching
the floor, and if I try a laugh
that ripples green with mystery;
maybe he'll forget it's just me
hiding inside.

Silence Like Cool Sand

First lie in it.
Close your eyes.
Let it move through you.
Rock your shoulders back and forth.
Dig your heels in.
Slow your breath.

Curl forward and wash
your hands with it.
Pour it slowly on your legs.
Rub your heels deeper
into the damp.
Bury your toes.
Roll back, eyes shut.
Disappear into it.
Listen to the scratchings, then listen,
listen to free rhythms play.

Ode to Pizza

Yeast pillow
sailing
through the green
oregano air, floats
down into the bubbling
rumors of tomatoes,
the gossip
of basil and bay leaves,
stretches at the red
aromatic massage,
dreams in layers
of mozzarella, the black
oval dozings of olives
humming in the sun,
dough that naps
in the glow
of laughter,
round appetite,
cicular carpet
shrugging
at knives and forks,
tattles
in many tongues,
international traveler
riding red pepper cloud-currents,
cruising the seas,
rising
to grins
that pull the melted
cheese, *queso, fromage, kaas, ser, keshi, ocha,*
queijo, käse, panir, nailao, queixo,
formatge, brinzeu, cascaval, bú, formagio

from country
to country,
wrapping around us and
our gold floating globe.

Line 30: Cheese as spoken in, respectively, Spanish, French, Dutch, Polish, Papiamentu, Japanese, Portugese, German, Hindi, Mandarin, Galician, Catalan, Romanian, Turkish, Vietnamese, and Italian.

For Georgia O'Keeffe

I want

to walk
with you
on my Texas desert,
to stand near
you straight
as a Spanish Dagger,
to see your fingers
pick a bone bouquet
touching life
where I touch death,
to hold a warm, white
pelvis up
to the glaring sun
and see
your red-blue world,
to feel you touch
my eyes
as you touch canvas

to unfold
giant blooms.

Title: American artist (1887-1986) especially famed for her paintings of flowers
and Southwestern landscapes.

Line 7: The yucca or agave plant.

The Young Sor Juana

I

I'm three and cannot play away my days
to suit my sweet *mamá.* Sleep well, my dolls,
for I must run to school behind my sister's frowns.
She knows my secret wish to stretch. If only
I were taller. If only I could tell Mamá why
I must go, my words irresistible as roses.

My sister hears my tiptoes, knows her shadow
has my face. I tiptoe on, for I must learn
to unknit words and letters, to knit them new
with my own hand. Like playful morning birds
the big girls giggle, at me, the little tagalong.
I hear the grumble of my sister's frown.

I stretch to peak inside, to see
the teacher's face. How it must glow with
knowledge. Like the sun. A woman so wise
has never tasted cheese. She sees my eyes
and finally seats me near. My stubborn legs
and toes refuse to reach the floor.

At noon I chew my bread. Others eat soft
cheese. I've heard it dulls the wits. I shut
my lips to it. I must confess, when tired,
I slowly smell the milky moons, like Mamá
savors the aroma of warm roses. I linger,
imagine my teeth sinking into the warm softness.

II

I'm seven and beg to leave my sweet *mamá,*
to hide myself inside boys' pants and shirt,
to tuck my long, dark hair inside a cap
so I can stride into large cities, into their
classrooms, into ideas crackling
and breathing lightning.

Instead of striding I must hide from frowns,
from dark clouds in the eyes of my *mamá.*
I hide in my grandfather's books, sink
into the yellowed pages, richer than cheese.
Finally Mamá releases me to her sister.
I journey to the city. If only I were taller.

III

I'm sixteen and spinning in the glare of Latin
grammar. I cannot look away. Beware,
slow wits, I keep my scissors close,
their cold, hard lips ready to sink into
this dark, soft hair, punish my empty head,
unless it learns on time.

I'll set the pace and if I fail, I'll hack and
slash again until I learn. I'll pull and cut,
this foolish lushness. Again I'll feel my hair
rain softly on my clothes, gather
in a gleaming puddle at my feet.
My hands are strong, and from within I rule.

Title: Sor Juana Inéz de la Cruz (1648?-1695) of Mexico, a brilliant and accomplished poet and writer. The religious title *sor* means sister, or nun.

The Desert Is My Mother

I say feed me.
She serves red prickly pear on a spiked cactus.

I say tease me.
She sprinkles raindrops in my face on a sunny day.

I say frighten me.
She shouts thunder, flashes lightning.

I say hold me.
She whispers, "Lie in my arms."

I say heal me.
She gives me chamomile, oregano, peppermint.

I say caress me.
She strokes my skin with her warm breath.

I say make me beautiful.
She offers turquoise for my fingers,
    a pink blossom for my hair.

I say sing to me.
She chants her windy songs.

I say teach me.
She blooms in the sun's glare,
    the snow's silence,
    the driest sand.

The desert is my mother.
El desierto es mi madre.
The desert is my strong mother.

El desierto es mi madre

Le digo, dame de comer.
Me sirve rojas tunas en nopal espinoso.

Le digo, juguetea conmigo.
Me salpica la cara con gotitas de lluvia en día asoleado.

Le digo, asústame.
Me grita con truenos y me tira relámpagos.

Le digo, abrázame.
Me susurra, "Acuéstate aquí."

Le digo, cúrame.
Me da manzanilla, orégano, yerbabuena.

Le digo, acaríciame.
Me roza la cara con su cálido aliento.

Le digo, hazme bella.
Me ofrece turquesa para mis dedos,
    una flor rosada para mi cabello.

Le digo, cántame.
Me arrulla con sus canciones de viento.

Le digo, enséñame.
Y florece en el brillo del sol,
    en el silencio de la nieve,
    en las arenas más secas.

El desierto es mi madre.

El desierto es mi madre poderosa.

Poinsettia

You grew green and ignored
wild in the rocky hills of Mexico
a common weed.
A brown-eyed boy
with no Christmas gift for the Virgin
picked you
though he wanted to blaze her shrine
with gold or silver or stars.
He carried you inside a dark adobe church
set you before a flickering candle
cried in shame at his poor offering.

That tear
stained your green leaves red.

Graduation Morning

She called him Lucero, morning star,
snared him with sweet coffee, pennies,
Mexican milk candy, brown bony hugs.

Through the years she'd cross the Río
Grande to clean his mother's home. *"Lucero,
mi lucero,"* she'd cry, when she'd see him
running toward her in the morning,
when she pulled stubborn cactus thorns
from his small hands, when she found him
hiding in the creosote.

Though she's small and thin,
black sweater, black scarf,
the boy in the white graduation robe
easily finds her at the back of the cathedral,
finds her amid the swirl of sparkling clothes,
finds her eyes.

Tears slide down her wrinkled cheeks.
Her eyes, *luceros*, stroke his face.

for Anthony

Family Ties

Though I shop for designer jeans,
uniforms make me smile.
Chalk-white uniforms in store windows remind
me of my grandmother who refused to learn English,
who laughed with the women from the canneries
when they all filled her small home with the smell of fish,
filled her hands with crumpled dollars in exchange
for the white garments piled in pale pink
boxes throughout the house.

My grandmother preferred to shop in the grocery stores,
preferred buying garlic, onion, chile, beans,
to buying me gifts of frilly blouses and barrettes,
hers a life of cooking, cleaning, selling.
But when I shyly showed my *abuelita*
my good report card or recited the Pledge of Allegiance,
my grandmother would smile and hand me a uniform,
never the right size, but a gift
I would add to the white stack
at the bottom of my closet.

for Teresa McKenna

Line 14: Grandmother.

22

University Avenue

We are the first
of our people to walk this path.
We move cautiously
unfamiliar with the sounds,
guides for those who follow.
Our people prepared us
with gifts from the land,
      fire
         herbs and song
hierbabuena soothes us into morning
rhythms hum in our blood
abrazos linger round our bodies
cuentos whisper lessons *en español.*
We do not travel alone.
Our people burn deep within us.

Line 9: Spearmint.
Line 11: Embraces, hugs.
Line 12: Stories, in Spanish.

Teenagers

One day they disappear
into their rooms.
Doors and lips shut,
and we become strangers
in our own home.

I pace the hall, hear whispers,
a code I knew but can't remember,
mouthed by mouths I taught to speak.

Years later the door opens.
I see faces I once held,
open as sunflowers in my hands. I see
familiar skin now stretched on long bodies
that move past me
glowing
almost like pearls.

Match

The flash
lights the wick
wax softens, melts

fire spreads
sparks a core
frees a spirit
to sing its quiet song.

Mothers and Daughters

The arm-in-arm-mother-daughter-stroll
in villages and shopping malls
evenings and weekends
the walk-talk slow,
arm-in-arm
      around the world.

Sometimes they feed one another
memories sweet as hot bread
and lemon tea. Sometimes it's mother-stories
the young one can't remember:

"When you were new, I'd nest you
in one arm, while I cooked,
whisper, what am I to do with you?"

Sometimes it's tug
-of-war that started in the womb
the fight for space
the sharp jab deep inside
as the weight shifts,
arm-in-arm
      around the world

always the bodytalk thick,
always the recipes
hints for feeding
more with less.

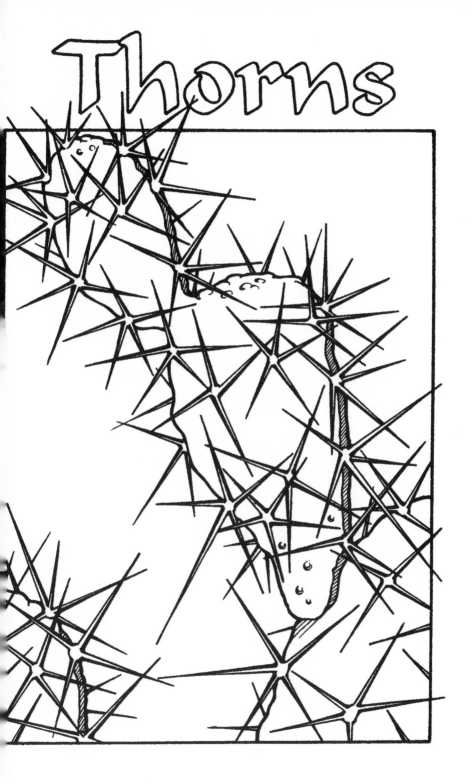

Picturesque: San Cristóbal de las Casas

No one told me about the bare feet.

The Indians, yes
the turquoise and pink shawls, yes
the men running lightly on thin sidewalks
hats streaming with ribbons, yes
the chatter of women sunning outside the church
weaving bracelets with quick fingers, yes

but no one told me about the bare feet.

The smiles, yes
the babies slung on women's backs,
the bundles of huge white lilies
carried to market: fresh headdresses,
the young girls like morning birds gathering
for a feeding, pressing dolls into my hands, yes

but no one told me about the bare feet.

The weavers, yes
the hands that read threads,
the golden strings pulled from bushes
in fresh handfuls to steal a yellow dye,
the houses in the clouds, in the high hills,
shuttles to-and-fro, to-and
-fro on tight looms, yes

but no one told me about the bare feet.
No one told me about the weaver's chair, a rock.
No one told me about the wood bundles bending
women's backs. No one told me about the children

who know to open their smiles
as they open their dry palms.

29

1910

In Mexico they bowed
their heads when she passed.
Timid villagers stepped aside
for the Judge's mother, Doña Luz,
who wore her black shawl, black
gloves whenever she left her home—
at the church, the *mercado*, and the *plaza*
in the cool evenings when she strolled
barely touching her son's wrist
with her fingertips,
who wore her black shawl, black
gloves in the carriage that took her
and her family to Juárez, border town, away
from Villa laughing at their terror when
he rode through the village shouting,
spitting dust,
who wore her black shawl, black
gloves when she crossed the Río Grande to
El Paso, her back straight, chin high
never watching her feet,
who wore her black shawl, black
gloves into Upton's Five-and-Dime,
who walked out, back straight, lips quivering,
and slowly removed her shawl and gloves,
placed them on the sidewalk with the other
shawls and shopping bags
"You Mexicans can't hide
things from me," Upton would say.
"Thieves. All thieves.
Let me see those hands."
who wore a black shawl, black
gloves the day she walked, chin high,
never watching her feet, on the black
beams and boards, still smoking
that had been Upton's Five-and-Dime.

Line 7: Marketplace.

Border Town: 1938

She counts cement cracks
little Esperanza with the long brown braids,
counts so as not to hear
the girls in the playground singing,
    "the farmer's in the dell,
    the farmer's in the dell,"
laughing and running round-round
while little Esperanza walks head down
eyes full of tears.
    "The nurse takes the child,"
but Esperanza walks alone across the loud
street, through the graveyard gates
down the dirt path, walks faster,
faster . . . away
from ghosts with long arms,
no "hi-ho the dairy-o" here,
runs to that other school
for Mexicans,
everyday wanting to stay close to home,
everyday wanting to be the farmer in the dell,
little Esperanza in the long brown braids
counts cement cracks

                          ocho, nueve, diez.

Fences

Mouths full of laughter,
the *turistas* come to the tall hotel
with suitcases full of dollars.

Every morning my brother makes
the cool beach sand new for them.
With a wooden board he smooths
away all footprints.

I peek through the cactus fence
and watch the women rub oil
sweeter that honey into their arms and legs
while their children jump waves
or sip drinks from long straws,
coconut white, mango yellow.

Once my little sister
ran barefoot across the hot sand
for a taste.

My mother roared like the ocean,
"No. No. It's their beach.
It's their beach."

Line 2: Tourists.

Peruvian Child

Still in the middle of my path is the child
with no smile who stared at us. Her eyes
even then the eyes of women who sell chickens
and onions in outdoor markets. The women
who stare at us as if we are guards.

She whispered to the doll with no face,
smoothed the red and blue scraps
of cloth on the path, ironed them with her hand,
wrapped and re-wrapped the doll, hair
mud-tangled as the child's, and the dog's,
and the llama's that followed the child's
small bare feet after she bundled the doll
in the striped *manta* on her back.

The matted group stood by the edge of the spring
watching us drink clear, holy water of the Inca,
a fountain of youth, our guide said.
We wanted, as usual, to hold a picture
of the child in a white border, not to hold her
mud-crusted hands or feet or face,
not to hold her, the child in our arms.

Line 13: Mantle.

Petals

have calloused her hands,
brightly colored crepe paper: turquoise,
yellow, magenta, she shapes
into large blooms for bargain-hunting tourists
who see her flowers, her puppets, her baskets,
but not her—small, gray-haired woman
wearing a white apron, who hides behind
blossoms in her stall at the market,
who sits and remembers collecting wildflowers
as a girl, climbing rocky Mexican hills
to fill a straw hat with soft blooms
which she'd stroke gently, over and over again
with her smooth fingertips.

Los pétalos

le han causado callos en las manos,
crepé de colores brillantes—turquesa,
amarillo, rosado—que ella transforma
en pétalos grandes para turistas comprando a lo barato
que ven sus flores, títeres, canastas
pero a ella no—canosa, diminuta
en su delantal blanco, escondiéndose detrás
del florecimiento en su puesto de mercado,
sentada recordando las florecitas silvestres que colectaba
de niña entre los cerros mexicanos
para llenar un sombrero de paja con flores delicadas
que frotaba suavemente una y otra vez
con las puntitas tiernas de los dedos.

Immigrants

wrap their babies in the American flag,
feed them mashed hotdogs and apple pie,
name them Bill and Daisy,
buy them blonde dolls that blink blue
eyes or a football and tiny cleats
before the baby can even walk,
speak to them in thick English,
     hallo, babee, hallo,
whisper in Spanish or Polish
when the babies sleep, whisper
in a dark parent bed, that dark
parent fear, "Will they like
our boy, our girl, our fine American
boy, our fine American girl?"

Los inmigrantes

envuelven a sus bebés en la bandera americana,
les sirven puré de *hot dog* y pastel de manzana,
los nombran Bill y Daisy,
les compran muñecas rubias que pestañean azules
ojos o una pelota de fútbol y tojinitos
antes de que el bebé ni pueda andar,
les hablan en un inglés espeso,
    alou, beibi, alou,
susurran en español o polaco
cuando los bebés duermen, susurran
en la oscura cama de los padres, el oscuro
temor de los padres—¿Querrán
a nuestro hijo, a nuestra hija, nuestro buen americano,
nuestra buena americana?

Abuelita's Ache

Celia watches him with the green eyes
of a woman in love, watches him laugh
and strut free through the market
a loose rooster sqawking
while her love grows tendrils
tangling inside her.

Blind old woman am I who didn't see
how carefully she braids her hair
now hoping to braid him
tight to her. And her morning face
pale as old sheets? And her loose clothes?
Blind old woman am I. *Ay. Ay. Ay.*

Village snakes will hiss-hiss,
"Celia's secret's blossoming, blossoming."
Each day I want to pile the vegetables we sell
higher and higher, to hide my sweet, foolish girl
in the green dark, to sing to her
like I did when I rocked her to sleep in my arms,
  rru-rru-que-rru-rru
lullabies she will need soon enough.

Title: Grandmother.

Two Worlds

Bi-lingual, Bi-cultural
able to slip from "How's life"
to *"M'estan volviendo loca,"*
able to sit in a paneled office
drafting memos in smooth English,
able to order in fluent Spanish
at a Mexican restaurant,
American but hyphenated,
viewed by anglos as perhaps exotic,
perhaps inferior, definitely different,
viewed by Mexicans as alien
(their eyes say, "You may speak
Spanish but you're not like me")
an American to Mexicans
a Mexican to Americans
a handy token
sliding back and forth
between the fringes of both worlds
by smiling
by masking the discomfort
of being pre-judged
Bi-laterally.

Line 3: They're driving me crazy.

Elena

My Spanish isn't enough.
I remember how I'd smile
listening to my little ones,
understanding every word they'd say,
their jokes, their songs, their plots.
   Vamos a pedirle dulces a mamá. Vamos.
But that was in Mexico.
Now my children go to American high schools.
They speak English. At night they sit around
the kitchen table, laugh with one another.
I stand by the stove and feel dumb, alone.
I bought a book to learn English.
My husband frowned, drank more beer.
My oldest said, "Mamá, he doesn't want you
to be smarter than he is." I'm forty,
embarrassed at mispronouncing words,
embarrassed at the laughter of my children,
the grocer, the mailman. Sometimes I take
my English book and lock myself in the bathroom,
say the thick words softly,
for if I stop trying, I will be deaf
when my children need my help.

Line 6: Let's go ask Mother for some candy.

Learning English: Chorus in Many Voices

i feel like a small child
only able to speak very simple
all the time i feel incomplete

when i have children they laugh maybe

i am trying to get out of ignorance
a hole so deep

there my mother a professional
here no job   no friends but still i see
strong woman goes to school does not care
that people laugh when she speaks

i am not shy just do not know
english my big problem i believe
i talk choppy
but want opportunity

my husband helps me

at my pronounce   mine sneers

mine an obstacle but
i never listen to him inside
i want my degree

i cannot understand
my tongue tied and nervous
ashamed i feel

i am old so sometimes disappointed
pessimistic of my english   i study
                                       i sometimes weep

my baby son three months   an american
will he tease his mother
who can not speak english so perfectly

      i am embarrassed
      almost every day
      why people so mean

I feel stupid
when i watch tv

      people still laugh at me
      when words stumble out
      i want to disappear

my child learns faster
how can i   what if we
use different languages some day
fat fear

      i feel a little burdensome
      much homework   teaching more fast here

it is not easy
in our new dream country
our language may not help our family

      broken my english
      but doing my best
      to express
      me

for the brave students who write me after reading "Elena"

42

Mush

"How's life?" The question tugs
him back. How long has he sat
at the kitchen table,
he wonders. He pours
himself into another glass, pats
his chest with his palm.

"It's my *corazón*," he says.
"I met a girl, so beautiful
I had to wear sunglasses
to look at her, and when her eyes
caught me, I felt dizzy, afraid
I might stop breathing.

"Before she left town, I told her,
had to, had to, but my words,
just mush in my mouth.
Later, alone, what I wrote sizzled,
like lightning, but
too late." He pours another glass.

"Here's her note. Before I opened it,
I wrote myself three versions.
Mine were better." He pours again,
gulps. "I feel sick, the ole *corazón,*
so I'm just drinking glass after
glass of water, until I feel like me."

Line 7: Heart.

43

Sugar

"¿Quieren una Coca?" My father's payday
question. We slam the doors of our squeaky
car and run into the store we pass daily
on the way home from the fields, hungry
for chocolate candy, cold drinks,
ice cream to melt in our dry mouths.

The store's shade cools me after a bent day.
The sun, a huge iron, pressed our backs.
Behind the counter, the man watches our
hands, empties our pockets with his eyes.
Why do we come here?

Without looking, I see
customers shrink from our brown skin.
I slide my hands deep in my pockets,
move away from my family, walk down
the aisles studying the chipped floor, hoping
my father won't lay his English, a broken puzzle,
on the plastic counter. Why do we come here?

"Peek un cahndee, Tonya," my father says,
my name that doesn't smell like Iowa,
where I was born. I reach for something
sweet on my tongue.
A woman with shoes white as her blouse,
a shiny woman, nudges her friend,
their eyes on my hands. "Dirty wetbacks,"
she whispers. "Look at them. Do you think they ever
bathe? The women just baby breeders. I hear
fifty of them live in one of those shacks."

I want to scream, "I belong here! I belong
here!" A scream bursting from my lips
smearing this dumb store with a smell
soap can't clean.
In the car, I try not to listen
to my family laughing while they rip open
the packaged sugar, stuff their mouths to forget.

I scrub her words away in the shower, scrub
my skin till it burns, let the water run
down my back and my dark American legs.

Line 1: Do you all want a Coke?

Same Song

While my sixteen-year-old son sleeps,
my twelve-year-old daughter
stumbles into the bathroom at six a.m.
plugs in the curling iron
squeezes into faded jeans
curls her hair carefully
strokes Aztec blue shadow on her eyelids
smooths Frosted Mauve blusher on her cheeks
outlines her mouth in Neon Pink
peers into the mirror, mirror on the wall
frowns at her face, her eyes, her skin,
not fair.

At night this daughter
stumbles off to bed at nine
eyes half-shut while my son
jogs a mile in the cold dark
then lifts weights in the garage
curls and bench presses
expanding biceps, triceps, pectorals,
one-handed push-ups, one hundred sit-ups
peers into the mirror, mirror and frowns too.

for Libby

No Substitutes

"Don't bother," I snap
and bang the door. Don't bother.
Skip the trip to the pound.

I'm trapped
in a pack of imbeciles.
Who wants *another* dog?

No substitutes, get it?
No imitations, no
fake leather, glass diamonds.

He was one of a kind.
The dog you called a mutt
understood what none of you
trapped in your gray mazes
can even imagine. He knew
me, get it?

I never had to explain why
I needed to pulverize the pavement
for hours or why I stare
out the window and forget
my name. He just panted
and followed my lead,
never pestered or nagged.

Maybe I'll just keep walking
until my feet wear out,
or I'll kick some dumb door
until I'm numb
and can't remember why I started.

Where does the bark go?

What did I bury?

To My Son

Such an empty backyard
without our worn swing set

          a clearing

leaving memories
with no bars to swing on

you

remember dangling bravely
upside down that Christmas

these last months chinning
that new long body
on those familiar bars
before you packed and left

              another clearing

a loud silence in this house

memories like our old swings
on howling nights clanging, clanging.

for Bill

Cissy in a Bonnet

You wore your brain backwards,
the bonnet you called your brain
at four years old, pulled the yellow
ties to frame your face, the floppy useless brim
bobbing behind your head as you ran free.

At fourteen you frown and turn
away from the pictures, and us.
"You let me look like that?" you ask
again marveling at the ineptitude of parents.

The bonnet travels with me
wherever I move, a nondisposable artifact
for your eventual backwards journey below
your bones, for the day you study the family
album and finger the bonnet alone, maybe
pull it on, the ties dangling foolishly
around your careful face, a yellow clue
as you search next in the mirror
for the girl who laughed with her clothes.

Maybe part of the journey is always backwards,
the careful brushing away of the layers,
personal archaeology, uncovering forgotten,
broken pieces, sifting even in our dreams
until we fit the jagged edges into round wholes
we cherish privately; and occasionally we
break the code, with our fingers read our early
symbols, reunite with the rare spirits we house.

Goblin

We laughed double that night,
a desert rain bursting down on us
after *Ghost Busters*, lightning
flashier than the show inside.
You pulled my hand gently
jumping puddles, tugging
"You can make it. Jump."
My eleven-year-old mothering me.

I saw a flash
    ghost of my future in slow
    motion, shaky and gray leaning
    on my red-haired daughter firm
    of hand, squeezing to keep me
    with her.

Busy in the present
tickled by the rain
and my shaky steps in high heels,
you missed my sneak preview, my spook.

When did your hand grow so?
Yesterday I hid it safe
in mine, squeezed and squeezed
when the wind gobbled my words.

Good-byes

How loud they are
our silent hugs
outroar the airport's blare

       heart to heart

we seek to hide
the sting of tears
      our insides
               out

spilling on smiles
we so long to invent.

Little troupers we
laugh and mouth
our studied lines

step apart deaf
from our heavy pulse.

for Mother

51

Tigua Elder

How do I tell my children:
there is worse than pain.

I bury pills.
Let my stomach burn.
I bury them in the sand by the window,
under the limp cactus.
Maybe it slipped into a long sleep instead of me.
I speak to my grandchildren in our language,
but they hear only television, radio
in every room, all day, all night.
They do not understand.

How do I tell my children:
forgetting is worse than pain, forgetting
stories old as the moon; owl, coyote,
snake weaving through the night like smoke,
forgetting the word for the Spirit,
waida, waida, the sound I hear in shells
and damp caves, forgetting the wind,
the necessary bending to her spring tantrums.

Afternoons I limp like a wounded horse
to the shade of the willow and wait for sunset,
for wind's breath, familiar, cool.
She eases this fire.

There is worse than pain.
There is forgetting
those are my eyes in the mirror.
There is forgetting my own true name.

Title: An American Indian people native to the southwestern United States.

Roots

Desert Women

Desert women know
about survival.
Fierce heat and cold
have burned and thickened
our skin. Like cactus
we've learned to hoard,
to sprout deep roots,
to seem asleep, yet wake
at the scent of softness
in the air, to hide
pain and loss by silence,
no branches wail
or whisper our sad songs
safe behind our thorns.

Don't be deceived.
When we bloom, we stun.

Tejedora maya

You too know the persistent buzz
of white space, stubborn as a fly,
the itch. My white is paper,
yours is cotton cloth you smooth
with rough palms in the shade of the old tree,
feel designs alive,
Braille we can't see,
butterflies, scorpions, snakes
darting and tumbling in your dreams
brushing the backs of your eyes
slither to your fingertips, dart
into red and black threads
    your hands, your mother's hands
    your grandmother's hands
unleash frogs and flowers
older than your bones.

Title: Mayan weaver.

Bribe

I hear Indian women
   chanting, chanting,
I see them long ago bribing
the desert with turquoise threads,
in the silent morning coolness,
kneeling, digging, burying
their offering in the Land
   chanting, chanting,
      Guide my hands, Mother,
      to weave singing birds,
      flowers rocking in the wind, to trap
      them on my cloth with a web of thin threads.

Secretly I scratch a hole in the desert
by my home. I bury a ballpoint pen
and lined yellow paper. Like the Indians
I ask the Land to smile on me, to croon
softly, to help me catch her music with words.

Leyenda

They say there was magic at Tula.
Seeds burst overnight.
Plants danced out of the ground.
By dawn, green leaves swayed.

At Tula the Toltecs
picked giant ears of corn.
Mounds of soft cornsilk
became mattresses and pillows
for small, sleepy heads.

They say at Tula the Toltecs
picked green cotton, red cotton.
In fields that were ribbons of color,
Indians harvested rainbows.

They built palaces of jade, turquoise,
gold. They made a castle
of gleaming quetzal plumage,
and when the wind blew
small green and red feathers
landed on Indian heads.

Title: Legend.

Abuelita Magic

The new mother cries with her baby
in the still desert night,
sits on the dirt floor of the two-room house,
rocks the angry bundle
tears sliding down her face.

The *abuelita* wakes, shakes her head,
finds a dried red chile,
slowly shakes the wrinkled pod
so the seeds rattle
                    ts . ss, ts . ss
The *abuelita*
                    ts . ss, ts . ss
gray-haired shaman
                    ts . ss, ts . ss
cures her two children
                    ts . ss
with sleep

Title: Grandmother.

Village Therapy

Sly grandmother waits until the family leaves,
peeks out the front door of her adobe home,
sees her children and grandchildren walking toward
their plot of land, another day of weeding.
Waiting is her game, waiting to fill the house
for the day with soft, cheerful companions,
baby chicks—*pollitos*—who peck the dirt floor
at her feet, peck the rice and corn she hides
for them, peck as she laments granddaughters who
wear jeans, who drink beer, who kiss men on the lips
in public. She grumbles, *"¡Ay, qué muchachas!"*
as she washes the dishes, as she waters her plants,
"¡Ay, qué muchachas!" as she cooks beans,
as she pats tortillas. In the late afternoon,
this mother hen with the long, gray braid
gathers her brood, patient listeners, sweeps them out.

In the evening, when the family argues,
when her granddaughters sigh, *"¡Ay, Mamá!"*
at requests for loose clothes, high collars,
shy bodies; Abuelita dozes, too tired
from her day of talking to say more.

Line 11: Oh, those girls!

Los ancianos

They hold hands
as they walk with slow steps.
Careful together they cross the plaza
both slightly stooped, bodies returning to the land,
he in faded khaki and straw hat,
she wrapped in soft clothes, black
rebozo round her head and shoulders.

Tourists in halter tops and shorts
pose by flame trees and fountains,
but the old couple walks step by step
on the edge.
Even in the heat, only their wrinkled
hands and face show. They know
of moving through a crowd at their own pace.

I watch him help her
off the curb and I smell love
like dried flowers, old love
of holding hands with one man for fifty years.

Title: The old ones.
Line 7: Shawl.

61

En la sangre

La niña con ojos cafés
y el abuelito con pelo blanco
bailan en la tarde silenciosa.
Castañetean los dedos
a un ritmo oído solamente
por los que aman.

In the Blood

The brown-eyed child
and the white-haired grandfather
dance in the silent afternoon.
They snap their fingers
to a rhythm only those
who love can hear.

Puesta del sol

The gray-haired woman wiped her hands on her apron,
lightly touched the worn wood counters of her kitchen
as cars sped on the dirt road outside her window,
cars of young men hot for Saturday night,
beer and laughter.

The woman pushed open her front screen door,
looked at the swirls of summer clouds,
slowly watered the plants growing in large tin cans,
said to her small granddaughter, *"M'ijita,*
such a gold time of day, bird songs, wind songs."

The *abuelita* smiled when in the last tin can
she found a geranium in bloom, wine bloom,
her wine on a Saturday night.

for my father

Title: Sunset.
Line 9: My little one (affectionate).
Line 11: Grandmother (affectionate).

64

Maestro

He hears her
when he bows.
Rows of hands clap
again and again he bows
to stage lights and upturned faces,
but he hears only his mother's voice

years ago in their small home
singing Mexican songs
one phrase at a time
while his father strummed the guitar
or picked the melody with quick fingertips.
Both cast their music in the air
for him to snare with his strings,
songs of *lunas* and *amor*
learned bit by bit.
She'd nod, smile, as his bow slid
note to note, then the trio
        voz, guitarra, violín
would blend again and again
to the last pure note
sweet on the tongue.

for Abraham Chávez

Line 14: Moons, love.
Line 18: Voice, guitar, violin.

Pushing 100

I'm eating ugly today, she says
as peas roll off her plate
when she struggles to cut her fried ham.

You're ninety-four, I say.
For the first time I take her knife
and fork and quickly cut her meat,
embarrassed at my agility.
We have reversed roles.
Once she sat patiently and watched me eat,
ordered for me. Spinster aunt, mothering.

Why do I stutter now, she asks
mouth quivering like a baby bird's.
I didn't used to. Now the words just don't
come out. Not in English. Not in Spanish.
It's because I don't practice anymore.
In my room alone, I don't talk.

You're ninety-four, I say
and she laughs, almost embarrassed
at her age.
When will I walk better, she asks
maybe I need vitamins.

You're ninety-four, I say.
Most people your age don't walk at all.
Most people don't live to be your age.

True, she says, and we walk slowly
away from Denny's, her favorite restaurant.
She's smiling, still savoring
the vegetable soup, peas, mashed potatoes
with gravy, ham, garlic bread,
chocolate Bavarian mint pie, two cups
of hot coffee.

Oral History

You're dead but your voice spins
out from tape cassettes, reels me
back to my child-bed, storytelling
in the dark. While my teenagers bend
to kiss me good-night, I'm lullaby-
rocked by your rhythms,
like a mother's heartbeat, familiar,
comforting old friends, stories
with names wearing high collars
like Nepomuceno and Anacleta
who walk in genteel shoes on the dirt
streets of tongue-twister towns

Cuauhtemoc and Cusihuirachic.
You're dead but you walk
and talk in my dreams
night after night we're together
you're savoring the taste of your stories
your face lively with life
not the gray, boney silhouette
breathing loudly in that pale
hospital room where I'd whisper

stop   stop

No. You're my grand wolf again
Lobo, as you dubbed yourself
when you claimed four of us
as your *lobitos,* little wolves
who even now curl round the memory
of you and rest peacefully
in your warmth.

Line 26: Wolf cubs.

Tomás Rivera

They knew so much, his hands
spoke of the journey from Crystal City
to Iowa, Michigan, Minnesota, year after year
dirt-dusted in fields and orchards,
his hands a pillow at night,
in bare, cold buildings,
family laughter his favorite blanket.

On slow days his hands
gathered books at city dumps,
saved like the memories of smiling
hard at that first grade teacher
and her noises in the other language
that didn't laugh like Spanish.

Those hands clenched in the dark
at *víboras, víboras* hissing
    we don't want you, you people have lice
as the school door slammed
but Tomás learned,
and his hands began to hold books
gently, with affection. He searched
for stories about his people and finally
gave their words sound, wrote the books
he didn't have, we didn't have.

And he graduated over and over
until one day he was Chancellor Rivera,
famous Chicano, too needed,
his hands too full of us
to sit alone and write green stories

alive with voices, "fiesta of the living,"
pressing, the present pressing
like the hands reaching out to him,
and he'd hug the small, brown hands,
his hands whispering his secret
        learn, learn
his face a wink, teasing out their smiles,
a face all could rest in,
like the cherries he picked, dark,
sweet, round a pit, tooth-breaker
for the unwary, the lazy, the cruel.

His hands knew about the harvest,
tasted the laborer's sweat in the sweet
cantaloupes he sliced, knew how to use
laughter to remove stubborn roots
of bitter weeds: prejudice, indifference,
the boy from Crystal City, Texas,
not a legend to be shelved,
but a man whose *abrazos* still warm
us yet say, "Now you."

Title: Texas-born educator and author (1935-1984) of the novel *Y no se lo
tragó la tierra.* (And the Earth Did Not Devour Him) and other works.
Line 15: Snakes.
Line 47: Hugs, embraces.

Strong Women

Some women hold me when I need to dream,
rock, rocked my first red anger through the night.
Strong women teach me courage to esteem,

to stand alone, like cactus, persevere
when cold frowns bite my bones and doubts incite.
Some women hold me when I need to dream.

They walk beside me on dark paths I fear,
guide with gold lanterns: stories they recite.
Strong women teach me courage to esteem.

They watch me stumble on new trails I clear.
In hope, feed me their faith, a warm delight.
Some women hold me when I need to dream.

In their safe arms, my visions reappear:
skyfire voices soar, blaze, night ignite.
Strong women teach me courage to esteem.

They sing brave women, sisters we revere
whose words seed bursts of light that us unite.
Some women hold me when I need to dream.
Strong women, teach me courage to esteem.

Señora X No More

Straight as a nun I sit.
My fingers foolish before paper and pen
hide in my palms. I hear the slow, accented echo
How are yu? I ahm fine. How are yu?
of the other women who clutch notebooks
and blush at their stiff lips resisting
sounds that float gracefully as
bubbles from their children's mouths.
My teacher bends over me, gently squeezes
my shoulders, the squeeze I give my sons,
hands louder than words.
She slides her arms around me:
a warm shawl, lifts my left arm
onto the cold, lined paper.
"Señora, don't let it slip away," she says
and opens the ugly, soap-wrinkled fingers
of my right hand with a pen like I pry open
the lips of a stubborn grandchild.
My hand cramps around the thin hardness.
"Let it breath," says this woman who knows
my hand and tongue knot, but she guides,
and I dig the tip of my pen into that white.
I carve my crooked name, and again at night
until my hand and arm are sore,
I carve my crooked name,
my name.

Gentle Communion

Even the long-dead are willing to move.
Without a word, she came with me from the desert.
Mornings she wanders through my rooms
making beds, folding socks.

Since she can't hear me anymore,
Mamande ignores the questions I never knew
to ask, about her younger days, her red
hair, the time she fell and broke her nose
in the snow. I will never know.

When I try to make her laugh,
to disprove her sad album face, she leaves
the room, resists me as she resisted
grinning for cameras, make-up, English.

While I write, she sits and prays,
feet apart, legs never crossed,
the blue housecoat buttoned high
as her hair dries white, girlish
around her head and shoulders.

She closes her eyes, bows her head,
and like a child presses her hands together,
her patient flesh steeple, the skin
worn, like the pages of her prayer book.

Sometimes I sit in her wide-armed
chair as I once sat in her lap.
Alone, we played a quiet I Spy.
She peeled grapes I still taste.

She removes the thin skin, places
the luminous coolness on my tongue.
I know not to bite or chew. I wait
for the thick melt,
our private green honey.

Foreign Spooks

Released full-blast into the autumn air
from trumpets, drums, flutes,
the sounds burst from my car like confetti
riding the first strong current.

The invisible imps from Peru, Spain,
Mexico grin as they spring from guitars,
harps, hand claps, and violins,

they stream across the flat fields of Ohio,
hide in the drafts of abandoned gray barns,
and the shutters of stern, white houses,

burrow into cold cow's ears and the crackle
of dry corn, in squirrel fur, pond ripple, tree gnarl,
owl hollow, until the wind sighs

and they open their wide, impudent
mouths, and together *con gusto*
startle sleeping farm wives,
sashaying raccoons, and even
the old harvest moon.

Line 15: With delight, with gusto.

A Voice

Even the lights on the stage unrelenting
as the desert sun couldn't hide the other
students, their eyes also unrelenting,
students who spoke English every night

as they ate their meat, potatoes, gravy.
Not you. In your house that smelled like
rose powder, you spoke Spanish formal
as your father, the judge without a courtroom

in the country he floated to in the dark
on a flatbed truck. He walked slow
as a hot river down the narrow hall
of your house. You never dared to race past him,

to say, "Please move," in the language
you learned effortlessly, as you learned to run,
the language forbidden at home, though your mother
said you learned it to fight with the neighbors.

You liked winning with words. You liked
writing speeches about patriotism and democracy.
You liked all the faces looking at you, all those eyes.
"How did I do it?" you ask me now. "How did I do it

when my parents didn't understand?"
The family story says your voice is the voice
of an aunt in Mexico, spunky as a peacock.
Family stories sing of what lives in the blood.

You told me only once about the time you went
to the state capitol, your family proud as if
you'd been named governor. But when you looked
around, the only Mexican in the auditorium,

you wanted to hide from those strange faces.
Their eyes were pinpricks, and you faked
hoarseness. You, who are never at a loss
for words, felt your breath stick in your throat

like an ice-cube. "I can't," you whispered.
"I can't." Yet you did. Not that day but years later.
You taught the four of us to speak up.
This is America, Mom. The undo-able is done

in the next generation. Your breath moves
through the family like the wind
moves through the trees.

Tree-Wisdom

Its steady claws dig
deep. Center it.
Ten of us can't budge
its weathered,
stubborn trunk.

Yet its limbs are moved by every brush of flesh,
feather, fur. Even a baby's breath starts a shiver
shimmering into the drowsy steam.
Those limbs, like moon-drunk flamenco gypsies, stretch
their gold, green, and garnet bangles into wind
wails, whirl wild when thunder claps.

Still, a tree moves, trembles
at the invisible. Without lungs or lips,
whispers and howls.

In wise rhythm, a tree retreats,
strips to feed itself.

But when the sap springs, a tree's bones burn
green. How it swells, then, a mass of praise.
A tree surprises itself, year after year,
climbs its rings,
climbs itself.

Bosque del Apache

if the earth's old bones smile
I hear them
in the hush of this greenless forest
shining up to the gray clump of salt cedar
    to black swords of mesquite
    to the grace of grasses, yellow, rust

    if the earth's old bones smile
I hear them shining
to strange chirps and chatters
to strange birds with necks that flow and flow
Canadian geese, sandhill cranes
stirring the air, stirring the air

    if the earth's old bones smile
I hear them shining
in pools, in the mallard's green shimmer
in the startled   FLAP
filling the blue with a whirl white
               silent, vast
then dip of black tip
        snow geese, snow geese

if the earth's old bones smile
I hear them
shining in the white of the majestic crane
the great Whoop
white neck flowing, flowing
into desert grasses
white flowing
into the smile of old bones.

Title: U.S. National Wildlife Refuge in New Mexico. The place name means
Apache Woods.

Senior Citizen Trio

They carry their words into the activity room,
scrubbed air, four walls bare of decoration,
no grace—but theirs. On sidewalk gray
January days, three students warm themselves
with coffee, survivors' smiles, and once-upon-
a-time Depression tales of empty pockets,
dinners of meat and potatoes, without the meat.

They read to one another, hands and words tremble
a bit, and then the catch in the throat, his tears
surprising them, and him. His apologies magnified
by hearing aids.

"I never thought I'd cry about it," he says.
"I was twelve then, so long ago, skinny kid
selling newspapers on a cold corner,
and Nini, my Italian friend, invited me
into his loud house. His family laughed at my
thin face, wedged me between thick shoulders
at the crowed table, gave me wine, a nickname,
spaghetti. At my Lútheran house, we never
drank, and we frowned at strangers."

He laughs, but his body cries again.
He apologizes, reads his last sentence,
"Thank God," but his body cries again,
"for Italians."

The two women know all about tears.
"Vell," says Helen who came from Hungary,
at forty, peeled grapes into fruit cocktail
while she learned English, "Vell," she says,
"You vere lucky."

Marty, one of eleven children who never saw
her mother's face, who brings the picture
of the daughter she buried last year, says,
"We won't live forever, ya know.
It's good to save the stories."

Now and Then, America

Who wants to rot
beneath dry, winter grass
in a numbered grave
in a numbered row
in a section labeled Eternal Peace
with neighbors plagued
by limp, plastic roses
springing from their toes?
Grant me a little life now and then, America.

Who wants to rot
as she marches through life
in a pin-striped suit
neck chained in a soft, silk bow
in step, in style, insane.
Let me in
to boardrooms wearing hot
colors, my hair long and free,
maybe speaking Spanish.
Risk my difference, my surprises.
Grant me a little life, America.

And when I die, plant *zempasúchitl*,
flowers of the dead, and at my head
plant organ cactus, green fleshy
fingers sprouting, like in Oaxaca.
Let desert creatures hide
in the orange blooms.
Let birds nest in the cactus stems.
Let me go knowing life
          flower and song
will continue right above my bones.

Line 21: Marigolds.